The Little Book of Self Leadership

Daily Self Leadership

Made Simple

Dave Williams

Published by SLR Coaching & Consulting Pty Ltd

First published 2017

Text and image copyright David Williams 2017

Design and typography by Logo Chap

This book is copyright. Apart from any use permitted under the Australian Copyright Act 1986 and subsequent amendments, no part may be produced, stored in a retrieval system or transmitted by any means or process whatsoever without the prior written permission of the author.

Where other sources are referenced, the author has ensured that the source is recognized so that readers may access the original work to further their knowledge and understanding.

ISBN: 978-0-6481801-1-4

ISBN: 978-0-6481801-1-1

David Williams, 1960 –

Contact: littlebookofselfleadership@gmail.com

Dedication

May there come a day when it's common sense that people treat their inner Parts as people, and that we consequently treat our children with even more calm, curiosity and compassion. And may that Self Leadership radiate across the generations and across our worlds.

Contents

Acknowledgements 6
About This Book 8
About The Author 10
Noticing My Parts Now 12
Parts Of Me Remember 14
Parts That Doubt 16
My Self 18
My Self Experienced 20
Speaking For My Parts 22
Personal Integrity And My Parts 24
S.I.F.T.'ing My Parts 26
Treating Your Parts as People 28
Respecting My Parts 30
Rejecting Restricts 32
The Most Powerful Question 36
My Exile Parts 40
My Protector Parts 44
My Manager Parts 48

Contents

My Fire Fighter Parts 50
The Self Leadership Model 54
Gaining My Protectors' Permission 58
Are My Parts Aware Of My Self? 62
Updating My Exiles 66
Witnessing My Exiles 70
Re-parenting My Exiles 74
Retrieving My Exiles 78
Locating My Exile's Burdens 82
Unburdening My Exiles 86
Reclaiming Disowned Qualities 90
Transforming My Protectors 94
Unburdening My Protectors 98
Rehearsing 102
Waking Up 106
Dreams 110
The Self Leadership Road Map 113

Acknowledgements

Reading about Internal Family Systems Therapy[1] (I.F.S.) was a light bulb moment. It crystalized my learnings from Psychodrama, Buddhist Meditation, Executive Coaching and Eye Movement Desensitization Reprocessing, into a simple accurate model and method. So a huge thank you goes to Dick Schwartz for having the insight and persistence to create and communicate Internal Family Systems.

Every book needs to be proof read again and again, and that task has been done with great care by my wife, Claire. More than that though, she has been a patient supporter throughout our adventure together, and for that I feel very grateful.

---

[1] Schwartz, R, (2001). *Introduction to the Internal Family Systems Model*, Oak Park: *Trailheads Publications*.

To my fellow practitioners who have listened to me enthuse about Self Leadership and its' potential to 'change the world.' Thank you for listening, challenging and contributing. Our conversations have helped enormously to rehearse how to more clearly articulate the I.F.S. concepts and Self Leadership experience.

Finally, I am indebted to my clients for trusting me to apply my skills as a Coach and Therapist to their inner world of Parts, and to gain that precious satisfaction that comes when someone's Self Leadership grows and empowers their lives, families and their careers to grow.

It's my hope that the Self Leadership that my clients and their children display in their communities will contribute over time to the evolution of an even more Self-Led World.

About This Book

For all the people who believe they are this 'sort of person', and wonder why, with particular people, in certain situations, they become someone else? This pithy little book is for you.

Part of you is reading this book right now, whilst another Part is probably thinking about all the other things you could be doing. Most of us live our lives unaware of which Part of us is taking the lead at any one particular time.

In this book, you'll have the opportunity to reconnect with your Self and re-establish your Self as the leader of your inner Parts. This shift in viewing your inner world as comprising 'Self' and 'Parts' is seismic and thus transformational.

Also, the pages are intended to be read in pairs. On the left-hand side page, you'll read poem-like accounts and instructions on how you can grow your Self Leadership. If that's too abstract, then you'll find an example on the right-handside page.

In our success obsessed Western culture, I've chosen an example of a person who has Parts that are driven to succeed, and yet remembers the discomfort of failing and fears failing again.

So, I hope you enjoy reawakening your Self and transforming your relationships with your Parts and the people around you. Because with a team of Self Led Parts within you, you'll find your life flows and fulfils. Here's to contributing to a Self Led World of curiosity, compassion, courage, creativity and confidence.

About The Author

Dave Williams is a registered Psychologist living in Sydney Australia who started his career working with leaders in the corporate world for 17 years. In the year 2000, Dave set up his own mentoring business, joint ventured with an executive coaching firm, and ever since has worked one-on-one with hundreds of leaders of Australian businesses, big and small.

In 2016, Dave read the book, *The Body Keeps the Score*, by Bessel Van derKolk[2]. It's here that Dave started his journey of understanding and applying Dick Schwartz's approach to Self Leadership. He realized that what he had been doing with his Comfort Zone Coaching was actually identifying what Schwartz called, inner 'Parts.' In particular, the Parts that his clients were uncomfortable with. By enabling his clients to step back from their Parts, Dave learnt that his coaching had been enabling people to lead from a place that Schwartz calls 'Self'.

---

[2]Van Der Kolk, B. (2015). The body keeps the score: New York: Penguin Books.

'Self' is that core sense of calm clarity within you that has the potential to lead the internal resources of your Parts with curiosity, compassion, courage, confidence and creativity. It's a presence that empowers any person to handle the highs and lows of life with greater ease and effectiveness.

So this book aims to enable you to be even more Self Led. And if through your example, others are inspired to learn and become more Self Led as well, then it is Dave's hope that in some small way, this book contributes to the evolution of an even more Self Led World.

You can contact Dave via:
dave@selfleadershipaustralia.com.au

Noticing My Parts Now

Part of me wants to read this book, another Part of me can't be bothered.

I'm recognizing the Parts that are within me right now.

Like the voice that says, 'I can', versus the voice that says, 'I can't.'

Whenever I say 'I'm struggling' with something, it's my Parts who are struggling.

Knowing my Parts makes life less of a struggle.

Knowing my Parts gives me more power and peace.

Example – Do You Have A Part?

Do you have a 'Driver Part' who says to you something like, 'I've got to do this', 'I want to achieve that', or 'I've got to work harder'? OR

An 'Indulgent' Part' who suggests to you, 'I'll do it later', 'Take it easy', 'Have a rest', 'Life's too short.' OR

A 'Fearful Part' who warns you about what could happen if you take on too much and says, 'I hate failing'. You could call that your 'Fear of Failure Part.'

It's common to have some Parts that argue with each other. Their arguing creates internal confusion, lowers your energy and erodes your capabilities to handle challenging situations. Next moment you hear yourself saying something like, 'I'm struggling with XYZ.' Go inside and see if it's really different Parts of you who are struggling?

Parts of Me Remember

We've all had our fingers burnt.

It might not be a big burn, but it did hurt.

Part of me remembers. It's happening inside me right now.

Other people may doubt it, but it's real for me.

Example – How do you relate this?

Do you have a Part of you that remembers doing something in front of people important to you and realizing they weren't responding to you the way you wanted? Were they staying silent, looking distracted, even frowning and whispering?

Suddenly your heart began to pound, or your voice got shaky, maybe you got tense in your stomach and unclear about what to say next.

Over time you develop a Part of you that fears you failing to get people to like what you've done (and to like you). That 'Fear of Failure' Part of you keeps a look out for situations where that could happen again, except now you're older and you've got to do presentations and projects in front of your boss, clients and colleagues all the time. That means your Fear of Failure Part is often the main Part in your life.

Parts that Doubt

All this talk about Parts. 'It's a bit weird. You're just imagining these Parts.'

So now I've got a Part that insists my other Parts aren't real.

Ah, that's my Skeptical Part. I almost missed that Part.

Hello Skeptical Part.

Example – How do you relate to this?

Have you ever had a Part of you that tells you the reason why someone is being 'nice' to you, is because they 'want something from you', not because they genuinely like you? Such a 'Distrusting Part' makes it harder to open up to people and build closer relationships.

How familiar are you with a Part of you that asks questions like, 'Why did you do that?' Or maybe you have a Part of you that tells you, 'You should have done this.' That's your 'Self-Critical Part' who makes you doubt your own capabilities and undermines your self-confidence.

My Self

Who's aware of my Parts?

Well I am. That's a stupid question.

Is it? Who's the 'I' that is aware?

That's my 'Self' who is aware of my Parts.

That awareness empowers my Self to lead my Parts.

To accept and welcome all my Parts.

And yet my Parts often take over my Self with their demands and emotions.

When that happens, I can't find my Self. I am the Part.

Example – How do you relate to this?

Talking to Yourself – Sometimes you may be aware of a conversation happening within you. Like the voice inside that asks, 'What are they thinking about me?' Another voice might say, 'I don't care what they think about me.' It's my Self who's curious to hear what my Parts are saying inside of me.

Looking in the Mirror – When you look in a mirror, you can do it a few ways. You can see that familiar face, brush your teeth and move on, or you can become aware of the Parts of you that judge the features on your face. Like the Critical Part who analyses your creases and blemishes for age, attractiveness, cleverness, health and happiness. And then there's the presence in the background who is aware of both that physical face and the mental commentary. My Self feels compassion for that person in the mirror.

My Self Experienced

What's my Self like?

Deep breath. Let me go inside and step back from what's happening inside me.

My Self is always there in the background. Timeless.

Has no colour, nor creed.

When I'm my Self, I feel calm and curious.

I look outwards with soft eyes and see clearly.

Alert, I'm ready to respond … effortlessly, creatively. No craving.

And I'm compassionate towards others - connected and separate at the same time.

My Self is the potential leader of my Parts.

Example – How do you relate to this?

Moments with Nature – When was the last time you stood beside a still lake, stared out to the horizon, or looked up at the stars and experienced that sense of vital stillness within you? In these sorts of moments, you are experiencing being in 'Self'. Spontaneously you become more calm, clear, confident and creative in handling whatever is happening within you and around you.

'In the Zone' – Have you ever done something really well without thinking about it? You probably weren't worrying about what could happen, nor were you going over what had happened in the past. You were most likely simply handling whatever was happening in front of you moment to moment - without a lot of thinking and effort. That was your Self in action.

Speaking for My Parts

Speaking for my Parts is a life skill.

I practice by saying, 'A part of me is ….'

And I notice there's 'Another part of me that is …'

There are Parts of me that are 'Frustrated', 'Flat', 'Vulnerable', 'Focused', 'Excited', 'Loving', 'Playful' and everything else in between.

Naming my Parts awakens my Self to 'unblend' from my Parts.

That's when I notice which Parts are running my life.

Examples – Do you relate to this?

Too Tired to Talk - You get home tired and your Partner wants to tell you about what has happened during their day. You say, 'A Part of me really would love to listen to you right now, and another Part of me is really tired and needs some quiet time before I can really listen to you. Can we talk in 30 minutes?

Getting Respect - Your Partner doesn't really listen to you and treat what you've go to say as important, so you say, 'A Part of me is feeling unimportant, and another Part of me wants to feel close to you. Can we talk?'

Handling Interruptions - A work colleague interrupts you, and you say, 'A Part of me really wants to help you, and another Part of me wants to get this task done that's due in 30 minutes. I could meet with you in an hour, how does that work for you?'

Personal Integrity and My Parts

When I say, 'A Part of me is feeling …' I accurately describe that Part.

No half-truths internally or externally.

No justifying, no gossiping, no blaming. My Parts are my responsibility.

By declaring my Parts, I own my Parts.

Making my Self whole, restoring my Integrity.

Examples – Do you relate to this?

Breaking Promises - Your phone rings and it's that person you promised to do that job for by yesterday. You haven't done it. You say, 'A Part of me feels guilty because I haven't done that for you yet. I really apologize for any hassles I've created for you. And another Part of me is committed to getting it done for you by today. Can that still work for you?'

Getting Hurt and Apologizing - One day you overheard this person saying you're not really honest. Instantly a Part of you feels hurt, quickly followed by another Part of you that wants to hurt that person back. And then your Self steps back and knows that retaliating will only further damage the relationship. So instead of blaming the other person, your Self shares with that person what each Part of you is feeling, and apologizes for any hurt you imagine you may have contributed to them experiencing. Regardless of how the other person reacts, admitting your contribution to the conflict makes you feel stronger on the inside.

S.I.F.T.'ing My Parts

Something or someone upsets me.

Something or someone excites me.

I S. I. F. T. each Part one at a time.

What … Sensations can I sense in and around my body?
  … Images appear?
  … Feelings arise?
  … Thoughts occur?

S. I. F. T.'ing my Parts fleshes them out.

Makes them more real and easier to relate to.

Example – How to you relate to this?

S. I. F. T'ing Your Self-Critical Part – Say you go inside and remember a time when you were critical of yourself. Start by scanning your body. You'll often be surprised that there are sensations that accompany the memory. Sensations such as a weight on your shoulders, or a tightness in your stomach. Because your Self-Critical Part has probably been with you for some time, it's common for images of other past events to appear. For example, your Self Critical Part may take on the appearance of someone who criticized you when you were younger. Then check what feelings the Part is experiencing? Perhaps it's fearing failing and anticipating the embarrassment of making mistakes in front of others. And what's the Part telling you? Is it telling you critical thoughts such as, 'That was stupid', 'Why did I do that?' By noticing the Sensations, Images, Feelings and Thoughts of a Part, you get to know your Parts much more fully.

Treating My Parts as People

My Parts have sensations, they see, feel, think.

My Parts remember the pain of the lows in my life. And they remember the highs as well.

My Parts act and react to other Parts and people around me.

My Parts act with a purpose. They take their jobs seriously.

My Parts look for someone to lead, be it my Self or a Part.

My Parts want someone to care for them, and to appreciate them.

Conclusion:
My Parts are a lot like people.

The more I treat my Parts like people living inside me, the easier it is for my Self to lead my Parts.

Example – How do you relate to this?

Do you have a Part of you who drives you to work hard to be successful? S. I. F. T. your 'Driver' Part and ask it, 'What are you concerned would happen if you didn't drive me to work so hard to succeed?' The answer will probably be that it's trying to protect you from experiencing the embarrassment of failing.

And if you ask your Driver Part, 'What's it been like for you to do that job for me?', you will mostly likely hear your Driver Part say something like, 'exhausting' and 'thankless'. What happens when you tell your Driver Part that you appreciate how hard it has been working to protect you from failing? Notice how much your Driver Part wants to be appreciated by your Self.

So your Driver Part is like a person living inside you who has sensations, thoughts, feelings, and a job to do. And like a person, your Self can talk with your Driver Part, express appreciation and develop a relationship with your Driver Part.

Respecting My Parts

The more I reject my Parts, the more they reject my Self.

The more I respect my Parts, the more they respect my Self.

How do I respect my Parts?

I respect my Parts by asking for their permission before I do things.

Like asking a Part, 'Is it OK if I speak to this other Part to get to know it?'

And I respect my Parts by thanking them for their commitment and cooperation.

Example – How do you relate to this?

Have you ever feared failing at something and so put it off? Go inside and S. I. F. T. the Part of you that fears failing.

Now ask your Self, 'How do I feel towards my Fear of Failure Part?' Many people say something like, 'I dislike it', or 'I resent it for holding me back'. The impact of these sorts of responses is that your Fear of Failure Part feels rejected.

Then ask your Fear of Failure Part, 'What's it like for you to be rejected by my Self?' Your Fear of Failure Part will probably ignore you or be just as resentful back. This counter reaction from your Fear of Failure Part demonstrates how rejecting your Parts, leads to more rejection and distance between your Self and your Parts.

Whereas if I ask my Fear of Failure Part, 'Would it be OK for me to get to know you?' Notice how differently your Fear of Failure Part responds.

Rejecting Restricts

I notice that when my Self doesn't lead, a Part of me takes over.

And when a Part takes over, I over or under react, which restricts my relationships and results.

And then I rationalize my suffering. I blame my Self, my other Parts, and the other people around me.

When was the last time I did that?

Example – How do you relate to this?

Have you ever got nervous giving a presentation? Perhaps you have a 'Failure Part' of you that remembers the embarrassment of having people in the audience whisper as you stumbled through your presentation.

You might recall the sensations of your heart pounding, a mental fog descending, and suddenly finding it difficult to remember what you were going to say next. In that moment, your Self was overwhelmed by the feelings of failure held by your Failure Part. You might have even stopped speaking.

Instantly your Fear of Failure Part rushes in to fill the leadership vacuum and urges you to take action, 'Leave the presentation!'. Anything to relieve the embarrassment of failing in public. The fear of experiencing the discomfort of failing only compounds your difficulty to speak fluently. Next your Driver Part kicks in to force you to read your presentation mechanically word for word.

But the audience can see these under and over reactions struggling within you. Your nervousness restricts your relationship with the audience as a credible source of information, which in turn restricts your capability to influence them to do what you want during and after your presentation.

A moment later you may have rationalized what happened by blaming your Self for not being there to calm and comfort your Failure Part. And so you start believing, 'I'm just not a confident presenter'. Or maybe you blamed the audience by thinking they were 'judging me' and 'closed to new ideas.' Or perhaps you blamed the world by believing it's 'risky', 'too materialistic', 'cut throat', and so on.

When you reject a Part, you instantly over and under react, which restricts your relationships and results, and then you rationalize why you did that by blaming your Self, other people and the world.

Parts I've Noticed, Promises I've Made

The Most Powerful Question

Self Leadership is more than a concept.

It's the felt connection between my Self and my Parts.

How I feel towards my Parts creates connection or disconnection.

Thus, the most powerful question I can ask my Self is, 'How do I feel towards this Part?'

Example – How do you relate to this?

It's relatively easy to intellectually understand that you have a Driver Part and a Fear of Failure Part, both of which aim to protect you from experiencing the embarrassment your Failure Part remembers when you failed at something.

But if you select one of those Parts and ask your Self, 'How do I feel towards this Part?' Your answer will uncover what type of connection or otherwise you have with that Part.

For example, you may appreciate your Driver Part for driving you to achieve more in your life, but also resent your Driver Part for not allowing you to be satisfied with what you have achieved and enjoy a rest sometimes. If you accept that your Driver Part has feelings, then imagine what it's like for your Driver Part to get this mixed message from your Self. Most likely your Driver Part is feeling confused and unappreciated for all the hard work it puts in to help you succeed and avoid failure. When you realize this is how you have been treating your Driver Part, your feelings may shift to having more gratitude and compassion for your Driver Part.

In which case, you could share these feelings with your Driver Part, and in all likelihood, you'll experience first-hand how your relationship with your Driver Part grows closer, which in turn affords your Self the opportunity to begin to be the leader of your Parts more often.

Parts I've Noticed, Promises I've Made

My Exile Parts

Parts of me remember when I got my 'fingers burnt'. From a little singe, to a big burn.

Events with waves of Sensations, Images, Feelings and Thoughts.

In an instant these waves can overwhelm my Self.

My Self becomes the discomfort, becomes the pain.

Let me see if I can step back and S. I. F. T. that Part.

The Part in pain so wants relief.

Other Parts rush to push the pain out of my consciousness, rejecting the Part and its discomfort.

If I was that Part that's in pain and I got rejected, how would I feel?

I imagine that Part feels lonely, neglected, abandoned, maybe even exiled.

How do I feel towards that Part now? Compassion wells up in me.

My Self is emerging, 'unblending' from my Parts.

Now I can see that the Parts whose discomfort I reject and push away are my *'Exile'* Parts.

Example – How do you relate to this?

Are you aware of a Part of you that has experienced failing at something? Usually it's when you were younger and more vulnerable than you are today. Perhaps you made a mistake in one of your first jobs? Maybe it happened on the sports field and you did something that lost the game. Or did you 'fail' an exam?

However you relate to these sorts of experiences, when you S. I. F. T. that Part of you that failed at something, you'll start to contact the visceral experience of failing. Perhaps you'll sense in your stomach the shame of making a 'fool' of yourself in front of others. You might also see images of a younger you trying unsuccessfully to participate. Those and other memories might trigger old feelings of inadequacy and powerlessness to change what you did and the consequences. You may also hear the Part thinking, 'I'm not smart enough', 'There's nothing I can do', 'I'm failing', 'I'm a failure'.

But no sooner than you start to experience the discomfort of your Failure Part, you'll probably get distracted by your Fear of Failure Part quickly jumping in with waves of fear that push aside those feelings of actually failing. Herein lies the problem. Too much fear makes it hard for you to think clearly, slows down your decisions, and makes your voice quiver. When that happens your Driver Part gets upset that you're not operating confidently, getting jobs done quickly, and looking successful. So your Driver Part tells your Failure Part it's not helping you to be successful and tries to control its feelings of failure by pushing them down.

So what's happened? Your Failure Part has been pushed aside by your Fear of Failure Part, and then criticized and controlled by your Driver Part. Given this, it makes sense that your Failure Part feels exiled from your other Parts and from your Self. Hence, you can call the Failure Part of you an 'Exile' Part.

My Protector Parts

Parts of me are really uncomfortable with discomfort.

Let me S. I. F. T. these Parts.

Like an over protective parent, these Parts keep watch for anything or anyone who might burn me again.

They insist, 'Never again!' and are so determined to keep me comfortable.

They make me baulk, blow up, binge, blank out, stay too busy.

They make me over and under react, stressing me and straining my relationships.

My Self asks the Part, 'What are you concerned would happen if you didn't do what you do?'

The Part is afraid and says, "Without me, you'd 'Lose it', 'Fall apart', 'Get hurt again', 'Die even.'"

Ah, so this Part is actually protecting my Self from being overwhelmed.

So even though these Parts restrict me - adding friction, creating fall outs, making me fail, I can appreciate how hard they work to protect me from continual discomfort.

These parts are really my 'Protector' Parts.

Example – How do you relate to this?

Say you have a Part that sometimes fears failure, or maybe you're aware of a Driver Part of you that drives you to work harder to succeed. Whichever Part you relate to, ask your Self, 'How am I feeling towards this Part?' If you are curious and compassionate for what that Part is experiencing, then ask the Part, 'What are you concerned would happen if you didn't do what you do?'

The answer will often be that the Part is striving to protect you from experiencing some sort of discomfort. The Fear of Failure Part will probably reply by saying something like, 'I keep watch for any risky situations where you could fail, and I protect you by making you avoid those situations.'

Meanwhile the Driver Part drives you to achieve success, so you'll never feel like a failure again. So both your Fear of Failure Part and your Driver Part are working to protect you from experiencing the discomfort of failing again. For this reason, you can categorize these two Parts as 'Protector Parts'.

And it's not always about the discomfort of failing. People experience countless types of discomfort, such as feeling hurt, helpless, weak, worthless, bad, abandoned, unloved, unimportant, stupid, vulnerable, to name a few. For example, you might have a Part that knows what it's like to feel hurt and helpless. In which case, you may have two Protector Parts. A 'Pleaser' Part, who works hard to make other people happy, and a 'Fighter' Part, who retaliates when people are perceived to have hurt you. Both Parts seek to protect you from feeling hurt. Indeed, just by taking the actions to please and retaliate, both these Parts also make you feel less helpless. Thus, both these Parts are examples of Protector Parts.

My Manager Parts

I notice how some of my Protectors want to control my other Parts.

They're telling me what I 'Have to' do, what I 'Shouldn't do'.

All to keep me from getting 'burnt' again.

I'll S. I. F. T. one of these Parts.

This Part is like a micro manager trying to keep my inner team under control.

Striving to protect my Self from being overwhelmed by the emotions of my other Parts.

Helping me cope with life's ups and downs. Focusing me on tasks that make me look good.

These are my 'Manager' Parts that my world approves of. Without my Self leading, my Manager Parts run my life.

Example – How do you relate to this?

If you have a Driver Part, then you'll probably be familiar with that voice in your head that tells you, 'I've got to work hard to succeed.' Why? Because basically it believes you're deficient in some way. Do you relate to having a Driver Part who believes you're 'lazy' and 'not smart enough' to be successful? In any case, your Driver Part probably believes you can overcome these deficiencies if you are focused, prioritize your tasks and avoid any distractions, such as fearing you might fail or doubting you could succeed.

In this way, your Driver Part works hard to control the degree of influence your Fear of Failure Part and Self-Critical Parts have over you. When your Driver Part is controlling your other Parts, you'll tend to project manage your life with task lists, work longer hours and find it difficult to switch off. Because this Part attempts to manage your other Parts, your Driver Part is an example of a 'Manager', which is a type of Protector Part.

My Fire Fighter Parts

Some of my Parts seem out of control.

Impulsive, inflicting pain on others, on my Self. Causing me crises.

They say, 'Go on, you deserve it', or 'Do it, they deserve it.'

The temporary relief they give me turns to feeling 'bad' and 'shame'. These are the Parts I hide.

Let me S. I. F. T. one of these Parts.

I ask the Part, 'What are you concerned would happen if you didn't do what you do?'

The Part answers, you'd feel, 'More frustration', 'More pain', 'Stuck', 'Powerless', 'Empty', 'Die even.'

Interesting, they honestly believe they're helping me. Giving me relief by distracting me.

Like a Fire Fighter hosing down my other Parts' emotions, this Part is unconcerned about the damage done in the process.

Wow! They're so courageous and committed to protecting my Self from discomfort.

Seen this way I can appreciate my *'Fire Fighter'* Parts.

Example – How do you relate to this?

Have you ever experienced a moment of fear that you might fail at doing something, particularly in front of a group of people? Maybe you've been invited to give a presentation but the size of audience was larger than you're used to, or perhaps you were contemplating getting married, or committing to do a challenging educational course, or a major project at work.

If you relate to these experiences, then you'll know the fear of failure is not a choice. It washes through your body in an instant, clouding your thoughts, slowing your decisions, and making your actions and voice shaky. When the audience sees you behaving nervously like this, unfortunately they start to think you're not very confident about your topic. Ironically, your Fear of Failure Part has made you more likely to fail to confidently do what you want and succeed.

And yet, if you ask your 'Fear of Failure' Part, 'What are you concerned would happen if you didn't make me so fearful of failing?' the answer you'll likely get is something like, 'If I didn't make you fear failing, then you'd get into more situations where you would fail, and you know how much you'd hate that!' In other words, even though your Fear of Failure Part sometimes restricts your capability to succeed, the Part genuinely believes it is protecting you from re-experiencing the discomfort of failing.

Importantly, you'll note that unlike the Driver Part, your Fear of Failure Part acts with an urgency to get relief as quickly as possible. Moreover, your Fear of Failure Part does this with little or no attempt to control the consequences of injecting such fear into your body. It's this combination of intending to protect you, whilst being unconcerned about controlling the costs to you, that are the key characteristics of what is termed, a 'Fire Fighter' type of Protector.

The Self Leadership Model

So when I go inside and take a deep breath, I notice there are three types of Parts within my Self.

There's my curious compassionate Self that's always there.

Calm and clear, my Self is the potential leader of my inner Parts.

But from an early age the pain of 'getting my fingers burnt' can overwhelm my Self, can make me cry and fall apart.

I can sense how I rejected the Parts of me that held that pain and so my 'Exile' Parts were created.

Naturally I feared getting hurt again, so two types of Protectors rushed to my defense. My Manager Parts, and my Fire Fighter Parts.

I can appreciate how hard my Manager Parts work to protect my Self by keeping my other Parts and their emotions under control.

And I can sense how my Firefighter Parts step in to distract me when there's an emotional emergency that threatens my Self and our survival.

Together my Self and these three types of Parts do what families do. Sometimes they're loving, sometimes they're warring, but always they impact my wellbeing and my world.

3 Types of Inner Parts[3]

Self

Managers
- Control

Protctors

Fire Fighters
- Out of Control

'Fingers Burnt'
Exiles

---

[3] Adapted from Schwartz, R, (2001). *Introduction to the Internal Family Systems Model,* Oak Park: Trailheads Publications.

Parts I've Noticed, Promises I've Made

Gaining My Protectors' Permission

Some days I'm aware of being upset with someone or something, including my Self sometimes.

Let me see, is it one of my Exile Parts that's upset?

Parts of me want to rush to my Exile's aid. Even my Self wants to help.

But my Protector Parts say, 'Hey! That's our job!'

Their whole purpose is to protect, so my Protectors worry, 'Are you trying to get rid of us?'

And my Skeptical Part chips in, 'You can try to help that Exile, but I doubt it will work.'

My Protectors' concerns won't go away.

The more concerned they are, the more my Protector Parts drive me to over and under react.

How can I reassure my Protectors? I know, I'll treat my Protectors like people.

I'll ask my Protectors' permission first, before I connect with my Exiles.

My Self asks my Protectors, 'Would you be OK with stepping aside for a while so I can get to know my Exile?'

I reassure my Protectors, 'You can come back if you think my Exile is getting out of control.'

My Protectors relax and allow my Self to connect with my Exile.

For without Protectors' permission, lasting progress isn't possible.

Example – How do you relate to this?

If you can relate to having a Part of you who knows the discomfort of failing, then it can be tempting for your Driver Part to attempt to 'make yourself' less fearful by telling your Failure Part to calm down. As admirable as this is, have you noticed how telling someone to calm down doesn't have a lasting effect? Why?

Even if your Driver Part gets busy doing calming exercises, your Fear of Failure Part is still left with its concerns about the situation and the potential to fail again. Indeed, your Fear of Failure Part may increase the intensity of its fears so that you can't ignore it. This in turn may remind your Failure Part what it feels like to fail, and thus undoes much of the calming 'work' your Driver Part has done.

It's a common vicious circle, where a Manager Part attempts to reduce an Exile Part's discomfort without asking a Fire Fighter's permission. This often triggers the Fire Fighter Part to intensify its' actions, which in turn re-activates the Exile's discomfort.

When you treat your Parts as people, you see the costs of ignoring your Parts and the importance of asking their permission before engaging with other Parts. In this instance, if you are feeling curious towards your Fear of Failure Part, then your Self could ask it, 'Would you be open to stepping aside temporarily so that I could get to know my Failure Part some more?' When your Fear of Failure Part agrees to step aside, then the relationship you build between your Self and your exiled Failure Part will be much more likely to grow and be supported by your other Parts.

Are my Parts Aware of my Self?

When I say, 'I'm so busy, I never get time by my Self.'

That's true. I'm too busy being my Busy Part to be my Self.

In fact, I wonder if my Parts are even aware of my Self?

I'll ask this Part, 'Are you aware of me?'

You're not?! How can I make this Part more aware of me?

What if I say to the Part, 'Hello?' What if I take a step closer? Reach out? Maybe make eye contact?

My Part isn't sure. My Self says, 'That's OK', 'I'm patient', 'I'm here', 'I'm interested', 'I care.'

My Part looks and responds, trusting my Self more.

Example – How do you relate to this?

A Manager Part of you can be so busy running your life that it's not even aware that your Self exists. If you relate to having a Driver Part of you, then pause a moment, S.I.F.T. your Driver Part, and ask your Driver Part, 'Are you aware of me?' You may be surprised to find your Driver Part is not even aware of your Self.

Similarly, you may have an Exile Part that has been so locked away from your day to day consciousness, that it has had very few interactions with your Self. When an Exile Part has been neglected like this, you may find that the Exile Part actively ignores your Self. Try this, let's say you have a Failure Part that holds the uncomfortable memories of past failures. S.I.F.T. your Failure Part and ask it, 'Are you aware of me?'

Having our Parts aware of your Self is fundamental to Self Leadership. You can make your Parts aware of your Self by treating your Parts as people with curiosity and compassion. Thus, if your Driver Part is concerned about you wasting its time and interfering with your other Parts, then you might invite your Driver to be more aware of you by reassuring it you won't waste its time, and that you won't engage with other Parts without first getting your Driver's permission.

Likewise, with a more vulnerable Failure Part, you may take a slower more sensitive approach towards raising the Part's awareness about your Self. Just as you would approach a vulnerable small child, so you might put your calm caring attention on your Failure Part, take a step closer, and perhaps gently say, 'Hello.' You may have to wait sometime before you get a response back from your Failure Part. The key is to care and be patient.

Parts I've Noticed, Promises I've Made

Updating My Exiles

I may not remember when a Part was created, but my Parts often do.

So I ask my Parts, 'How old are you?'

Their age tells me so much about my Parts' capabilities and the way they see the world.

I wonder how old this Part thinks I am?

So my Self asks the Part, 'How old do you think I am?'

Wow! The Part thinks my Self is a youngster.

No wonder my Parts don't trust my Self much.

I'll update my Parts and let them know all my grown up achievements and capabilities.

Example – How do you relate to this?

What you might refer to as the 'lows' in your life, are often moments when you were more vulnerable and your Self was challenged to handle the emotions that Parts of you were experiencing.

To illustrate, let's say you can remember a time when you were relatively young and you felt like you failed to give a successful presentation. In that moment when your embarrassment was most intense, your younger Self may have been temporarily overwhelmed by those feelings. Instead of your Self comforting the Part of you that felt like a failure, your Fear of Failure Part may have stepped in to keep you away from those sorts of situations in the future. Because your Fear of Failure Part keeps referencing to the past by ensuring that 'never happens again', it's understandable that your Fear of Failure Part sees your Self as having the capabilities that you had when you were younger.

Accordingly, it is often effective for your Self to be curious about how old a Part sees your Self. You can do this right now simply by asking a Part of you, 'How old do you think I am?' If you discover the Part believes you have the capabilities of when you were younger, then take your time explaining to the Part all that has happened since. Outline the personal qualities and skills you have developed and describe what you have achieved along the way. In brief, update your Part so that it gets to know your Self as you are today.

Parts I've Noticed, Promises I've Made

Witnessing my Exiles

Without my Self around, being a Part in discomfort is a lonely experience.

Only the Part of me experiencing the discomfort really knows what it's like.

So it's natural that my Parts want to share their discomfort with my Self.

To let me know what the Part experienced.

But without my Self's compassion and acceptance, my Part hesitates to open up.

It takes guts for my Part to share with my Self.

Memories pop up. Showing me what the Part went through.

My Part wants my Self to truly understand what it was like. I get it now.

Example – How do you relate to this?

People say, 'I hate this', 'I hate that.' Maybe you've heard someone say, 'I hate giving presentations.' What they're really saying is they hate the discomfort they experience when they give presentations. More precisely, what they're hating is the Part of them that is experiencing that discomfort. Imagine being that Part of you that is being told that, 'I hate you.' It's this type of rejection and isolation that our Exile Parts experience daily.

Do you know what you hate? If you S.I.F.T. the Part of you that remembers 'failing' at something, often you'll find that memories of when you failed spontaneously emerge. Perhaps the time you presented to your class mates and they snickered and mimicked you. Maybe you recall other more recent memories such as giving that 'bad' presentation at work. Each memory intensifying the sensations, images, feelings and thoughts your Failure Part carries.

It's understandable then that after years of being exiled, your Failure Part is keen to share this load with your Self. At the same time, your Failure Part may be cautious to trust that you won't just reject it like you may have done before. To earn this trust, your Failure Part may want your Self to really experience what it felt like to fail. In these moments, you'll probably start to experience uncomfortable sensations and feelings within you. If you allow your Self to be overwhelmed by these feelings, then your Self will become the Failure Part. The solution is to locate your Self in the scene of the memory your Failure Part is showing you. This enables your Self to be there as a separate compassionate presence who is supporting your Failure Part to handle what happened. This is why witnessing what your Parts went through is such an important step in your Self Leadership journey.

Parts I've Noticed, Promises I've Made

Re-parenting My Exiles

When my Parts trust that they can be vulnerable with my Self.

They show me what happened. Unconscious memories become conscious.

Scenes emerge. He said this, she said that. Sensations spark.

Feelings of unfairness, frustration, sadness and self-blame arise.

My Self feels compassion for my Part. The past suffering subtly continues to this day, now.

From the calm of compassion, my Self asks the Part, 'Would you like me to join you?'

I enter the scene. My Self and my Part in that most uncomfortable moment.

Gently my Self asks, 'What would you have liked to have happened?'

That something the Part always wanted to do, always wanted to say, but didn't.

My Self offers the Part a choice. 'Do you want to take that action or would you like my Self to do it on your behalf?'

The events are rewound. Seeing, hearing, feeling and sensing the moment of injustice.

Self and Part completing the actions that were left incomplete. Saying what was withheld.

Generating a visceral freedom that heals and transforms my Part.

Example – How do you relate to this?

Whatever memories you may have of failing at something, see if you can get a sense of the Part of you that remembers what happened. Then ask your Self, 'How am I feeling towards this Part that experienced failing?' If you are curious and compassionate towards your Failure Part, then have your Self enter the scene where the failure occurred so that you're with your Failure Part as the events unfold.

As your Self witnesses the image of a younger you bravely doing your best to give that presentation, perhaps you become aware of how your Failure Part withheld a rush of resentment towards the 'judging' audience - be they your younger classmates, or older work colleagues. At which point, your Self could ask your Failure Part, 'What would you have liked to have happened?'. Your Failure Part might respond, 'I want to tell them, that making fun of someone who's trying their best is not OK, and to show them how much they affected my confidence. Most of all, I want them to apologize for what they did!' Listening with compassion, your Self accepts that this is your Failure Part's truth.

Now your Self can ask your Failure Part, 'Do you want to say that to your classmates/colleagues, or would you like my Self to do it on your behalf?' Either way, your Failure Part gets to experience having your Self provide the type of support that was absent when the events occurred. This experience empowers your Failure Part to know it can rely upon your Self to provide such support in future situations. Your Failure Part is no longer exiled and alone.

Retrieving My Exiles

With my Exile now trusting my Self that I will be there as a calm source of compassion, comfort, support and safety.

My Self asks my Exile to travel out of the old scene where it got burnt.

To come out of the past pain and trust my Self just as I am now.

To be with my Self somewhere safe, somewhere comfortable.

Retrieving my Exile. Freeing my Exile from those memories.

No longer referencing what's happening with what happened.

So that my Part is with me now. Trusting to be in my Self's care.

Ready to handle today's challenges with fresh wisdom and finesse.

Example – How do you relate to this?

Even though your Failure Part may have accepted your Self's support to take corrective actions that completed what happened in those past failures, your Failure Part may still occasionally reference what it sees happening now in terms of what happened in the past. The next step in your journey of Self Leadership, therefore, is for your Self to invite your Failure Part to move out of the old scene where the 'failure' occurred.

Your Self can do this by asking your Failure Part, 'Would you like to leave this old situation and join me in the present?' Sometimes your exiled Parts hesitate because they still doubt whether your Self will really be there to support them when the next challenge arises. In which case, have your Self give whatever reassurances and promises your Failure Part needs.

When your Failure Part is ready to join your Self in the present, then repeat your invitation and do whatever is appropriate to join the Failure Part and travel to the present time. For many this means their Self takes their exiled Part by the hand, and within your inner world, travel to where you are now. Sometimes the current situation doesn't feel safe, so your Failure Part may decide to travel to an imaginary place where your Self and your Part are comfortable. This may occur quickly or slowly, the emphasis is on your Failure Part and your Self to experience the retrieval as viscerally real.

Parts I've Noticed, Promises I've Made

Locating My Exile's Burdens

Even though my Exile is with my Self now, safer and happier.

I sense in my Exile's little body, a weight. A burden of beliefs and feelings forged from past pain.

Beliefs that seemed so real to my younger more vulnerable Exile, so essential to survival, now exposed as past their use by date.

Like the burden of responsibility that weighs heavily on the shoulders of some Exiles.

Or the burden of not being good enough that stays in some Exiles' yearning hearts.

My Self scans my Exile's body, sensing the burden. Asking my Exile, 'Where do you hold those old burdens of beliefs in or on your body?'

My Exile answers. Found it. This is the first step to unburdening my Exile.

Example – How do you relate to this?

If you can recall a time when you felt you failed at something, then you can probably also recall what you believed about yourself and the other people at the time.

Returning to the example of failing to give a successful presentation, you might relate to thinking something like, 'I'm a failure', that 'I'm just not a confident person.' Your Self could be curious and ask the Part, 'What is it about you that makes you a failure and not confident?' This is where you may discover that at its core, your Failure Part believes, 'I'm not enough', 'not smart enough', 'not skinny enough', 'not strong enough' etc.

Because these beliefs are so closely associated with the visceral experience of those past failures, these beliefs are often carried like 'burdens' in or on your Failure Part's body.

Check this out for yourself. If you have retrieved your Failure Part from the old scenes where you failed at something, then ask your Failure Part, 'Where do you hold those old beliefs about yourself and the people present at the time? Where do you carry those old beliefs in or on your body?' Your Failure Part might respond, 'I feel the sense of not being confident as a tension in the pit of my stomach', and as a 'twitching in my right leg, like it wants to run away.' In this way, you can locate where your Exiled Part is carrying its old burdens of beliefs and the associated uncomfortable feelings.

Parts I've Noticed, Promises I've Made

Unburdening my Exiles

When my Exile has told me where those outdated beliefs are held in or on its' body.

I invite my Exile, 'Would you like to release the burden of those old beliefs?'

Any hesitation I sense and ask my Exile, 'What would be your concerns if you didn't release your burdens?'

I reassure my Exile and repeat my invitation to release those burdens into the elements.

A visceral release from my Exile's body into the wind … water … earth … fire … light … into the universe.

My Self encouraging my Exile to experience the unburdening completely.

Releasing the burdens forever. Experiencing the relief, lightness and freedom when the unburdening is done.

Example – How do you relate to this?

Let's say you have identified that your Failure Part carries the beliefs that 'I am a failure' because basically you're 'not smart enough to be a confident person and succeed.' And let's say that you can sense that your Failure Part holds these old beliefs as a tense stomach and twitching right leg. With enough trust and compassion, your Self can ask your Failure Part, 'Would you like to release the burden of those old beliefs?'

As your Self listens, you might detect some reluctance. That's understandable. Those old beliefs that your Failure Part is holding on to, not only explained what happened, they also gave your Failure Part's its identity and view of the world as being a 'risky place.' No wonder you need to reassure your Failure Part that your Self will be there to support it through any future situations that look like risking failure.

Only when your Failure Part is reassured and ready, does your Self ask your Failure Part to focus on the old beliefs and the sensations in its stomach and leg, and then in its own way, to release the burden of those beliefs into the wind, water, earth, fire, light, or universe. Wherever your Failure Part wants to send those beliefs, so that they are gone forever. As your Self waits patiently for your Failure Part to unburden the old beliefs, you may also experience subtle yet significant shifts within your body. Sensations such as relief, lightness, calm, completion, and a freedom for your Failure Part and your Self to express themselves with greater ease and spontaneity.

Parts I've Noticed, Promises I've Made

Reclaiming Disowned Qualities

It's subtle. By carrying those old burdens of beliefs, my Exile sacrificed other personal qualities.

Like taking on being so focused and responsible, that it's not OK to be fun and playful sometimes.

Or being too diplomatic, too sensitive, at the expense of speaking up and being strong sometimes.

Or having to be really attractive and active, because it feels lazy to have a rest and reflect occasionally.

Unburdened, my Exiles see the sacrifices made.

So my Self asks my Exile, 'What qualities did you give up back then that you'd like to reclaim now?'

Qualities like playfulness, confidence, creativity, kindness, assertiveness, openness … and the like.

I await the answer and invite my Exile to reclaim those personal qualities.

To absorb them and experience the visceral wholeness of reuniting with those reclaimed qualities.

Example – How do you relate to this?

By believing you are a certain type of person, you simultaneously take on particular personal qualities and sacrifice certain others.

For example, let's say you relate to having a Failure Part. When that Part of you started to believe that you're not very confident and not enough in some way, your Failure Part may have adopted qualities such as being cautious, nervous, shy and the like. In the process, your Failure Part may have also given up qualities such as being innovative and assertive.

So whilst unburdening the old beliefs will have freed up your Failure Part to grow in confidence, your Self can now ask your Failure Part, 'What qualities did you give up back then that you'd like to reclaim now?'

Unlike the unburdening, this time your Self is encouraging your Failure Part to viscerally experience what it feels like to have these personal qualities enter and integrate with your Failure Part's body. In this way, your Failure Part remembers the feeling of being innovative and assertive with other people. Memories of these experiences may pop up in your mind. Your Self can even invite your Failure Part to imagine having these personal qualities whilst doing something like a future presentation. Thereby experiencing the powerful combination of being confident, innovative and assertive.

Transforming My Protectors

I give my Protector the respect of asking, 'Are you aware of what has happened between my Self and my Exile?'

That my Exile is now trusting my Self to be there. To care and protect my Exile.

So my Self asks my Protector, 'With my Self protecting my Exile now, what role would you like to play?'

I reassure my Protector, 'This is not about getting rid of you. It's about inviting you to contribute in a new way that gives you a rest.'

My Protector likes that idea and starts imagining.

Like the Protector that chose to go from being a Self Critic, to Inner Consultant, or Slave Driver to a Prioritizer.

My Protector and Self settle on a new role that supports my Self to lead and grow.

Example – How do you relate to this?

It's easy to assume that each of your Parts instantly knows what your other Parts are doing. But like people, some of your Parts don't listen or talk much to each other. Indeed, because of the discomfort held by your Exiled Parts, they are often deliberately excluded.

It's possible therefore for your Self to have witnessed, retrieved and unburdened your exiled Failure Part, only to discover that your protective Driver and Fear of Failure Parts are not aware of what has happened. In which case, your Self can ask your Driver and Fear of Failure Parts, 'Are you aware of what has happened between my Self and my Failure Part?' If they aren't aware, then your Self can walk them through the steps your Self took to become the primary caretaker and leader of your Failure Part.

Often protective Parts like your Driver and Fear of Failure Parts are skeptical of your Self's capability to perform this new leadership role reliably. However, by reassuring them of your capability and commitment to care for your Failure Part, your Driver and Fear of Failure Parts will come to acknowledge your Self as the primary caretaker of your Failure Part. This opens the opportunity for your Self to ask your Driver Part and Fear of Failure Part in turn, 'With my Self protecting my Failure Part now, what role would you like to play?'

Frequently, Protector Parts hear such invitations as attempts to get rid of them. If so, your Self can reassure them by saying something like, 'This is not about getting rid of you. It's about inviting you to contribute in a new way that gives you a rest from protecting my Failure Part.' With these reassurances, your Self can engage your Driver Part and Fear of Failure Part in a dialogue that retains each of their best attributes in a way that supports your Self to lead your inner Parts and your life. By this means, your Driver Part might elect to become your 'Prioritizer' Part, while your

Fear of Failure Part might resolve to be your 'Assessor' Part. This transforms the excesses of your old Protector Parts into Parts that contribute to your Self's capability to be the leader of your inner Parts and your life.

Unburdening My Protectors

When I hear a Part say, 'I have to', 'I must', I know a Part is carrying a burden.

So many Managers carry the weight of 'having to' be responsible, good, perfect, beautiful etc.

Constantly putting up walls, analyzing, anticipating, rehearsing. It's a big job for a Part.

So many Firefighters 'must' get relief, get even, get off. Now!

Like a tightly wound spring. All that tension takes its toll.

But why? With my Exile in my Self's care and unburdened, there's less need to protect.

So my Self asks each Protector a series of questions.

'What beliefs and feelings are you carrying?' My Self listens openly.

And, 'Where do you carry those old beliefs and feelings? Where in or on your body?'

And, 'Would you like to release those old beliefs and feelings? So that you get a well-earned rest.'

'Yes', I hear my Protector say.

My Self asks my Protector, 'OK, so where do you want to release those old beliefs and feelings? Into the water, the wind, the earth, the light, perhaps the fire, maybe the universe? Wherever, forever.'

My Protector lightens that emotional load, discharging that spark that drives me to over or under react.

A visceral release experienced completely. Returning clarity and choice to my unburdened Protector.

Enabling me to adapt appropriately to that particular person, to that certain situation.

Example – How do you relate to this?

If you've been on this Self Leadership journey this far, then by now your Driver Part is supporting your Self more as your Prioritizer, and your Fear of Failure Part has become more your Assessor.

And yet there still may be times when your Prioritizer Part sometimes gets the urge to treat you as being lazy. Similarly, your Assessor may occasionally mistake a person's laughter as mocking, losing that valuable objectivity to assess the risks and benefits of each scenario. So long as these Parts continue to believe that you are 'lazy', and that 'people are cruel', then their transformation will not be complete.

So as with your exiled Failure Part, your Self can invite your Protector Parts to release the burden of carrying those outdated beliefs. Your Self can start by asking each of your Protector Parts, 'What beliefs and feelings are you carrying?'

In this example, your Prioritizer Part is likely to answer that it believes 'you're lazy', whilst your

Fear of Failure Part sees 'people as cruel.'

Next your Self can ask each Protector Part, 'Where do you carry those old beliefs and feelings? Where in or on your body?' It's amazing how readily your Parts relate to carrying these beliefs as burdens, such as a weight, tension or pressure in or on different parts of their body.

Then your Self can ask, 'Would you like to release those old beliefs and feelings, so that you get a well-earned rest?' With each Part's agreement, your Self may then ask, 'OK, so where do you want to release those old beliefs and feelings? Into the water, the wind, the earth, the light, perhaps the fire, maybe the universe? Wherever, forever.'

As each Protector releases the burden of their beliefs, it's likely that you also will feel a lightening of the emotional load in your own body. Feeling calmer, lighter, even joy.

Rehearsing

Let's see how this Self Leadership stuff works in practice.

I've got this situation coming up, similar to when I got my fingers burnt.

When I imagine the place, the people, the issue, what Parts come up? I S. I. F. T. my Parts.

How do I feel towards each of these Parts? Am I curious and compassionate, or critical and rejecting?

I pick a Part to connect with. What would it be like for that Part to hear my critical rejecting words?

My Self feels compassion for the Part, and says as much to my Part, apologizing.

My Part is trusting me more, relaxing. Allowing my Self to take the lead of caring for my Part.

We return to the place and people that are coming up, my Self with my Part.

We focus on the moment my Part anticipates will be the most unwanted and challenging.

My Self takes the initiative and comforts my Part.

Calming, supporting, trusting my Part to know how to contribute appropriately.

Umm, it's more of a dance. What I want is a given, not threatened. No need to defend, nothing to prove.

I'm free to adjust and enjoy every zig and zag of the encounter.

The more I feel the discomfort, the more I'm my Self, and the more effective I am.

Self Leadership makes my life less of a struggle, less stressful. And more fulfilling, and more fun!

Example – How do you relate to this?

Perhaps you can relate to knowing you have a presentation or project to do that stretches you somehow. Maybe there will be some important people watching you and relying on you to do a good job.

Take your Self to the moment that you anticipate will be the most challenging and uncomfortable. Now S. I. F. T. the Parts inside you that are active in that moment.

Ask your Self, 'How am I feeling towards each of these Parts?' Maybe you're most aware of your old Fear of Failure Part injecting a slight wave of fear through your body, making you a bit shaky. You catch a Part of you thinking, 'I don't like being out of control of this fear. I want it to go away.'

From all that you've learnt about Self Leadership, you know that rejecting a Part doesn't work, so you ask your Self, 'What would it be like for my old Fear of Failure Part to hear that I don't like what it's doing and that I want it to go away? You realize that your Fear of Failure Part probably feels like it is doing a thankless job trying to protect you from failing, without much recognition and support from your Self. A feeling of compassion and appreciation towards your Fear of Failure Part grows within you.

So you rewind to the most challenging moment, but this time with your Self standing beside your Fear of Failure Part providing words of encouragement and a calming presence. With your Self there, the world seems a less dangerous place, people are less of a threat, and somehow your Fear of Failure Part reclaims its capability to more clearly assess people, the risks and opportunities available in the situation. With your Self's support and leadership, your Fear of Failure Part has become your Assessor. You can see more clearly peoples' reactions, adapt more calmly and deliver more confidently what they want. People are pleased with what you did and say as much.

Waking Up

My eyes open to start another day.

My 'Got to go, go, go' Part kicks into gear.

But before my legs hit the floor, I hit the emotional pause button.

I S. I. F. T. my Parts and say a warm, 'Hello'.

Asking my Self, 'How do I feel towards this Part?', 'How do I feel towards that Part?'

Building my innate curiosity and compassion for each of my inner family of Parts.

Setting up my day to flow with Self Leadership.

Example – How do you relate to this?

In our busy lives it's easy to let certain Parts of us run our lives and lose our sense of Self. We all do this from time to time, so you'll find you benefit from establishing a regular practice of reconnecting with your Self and talking with your Parts with curiosity and compassion.

Your Driver, for example, may jump in as soon as you open your eyes in the morning and start reminding you about all the tasks you 'have to' get done today. It's so tempting to want to get straight out of bed and start 'doing.'

Whereas, what if you took one minute on your bed to S. I. F. T. the Parts there inside of you. Instantly you'll notice your Driver Part. Ask your Self, 'How am I feeling towards my Driver Part?' Perhaps you're sick of your Driver Part pushing you to achieve? Next you can ask your Self, 'What would it be like for my Driver Part to hear that I'm sick of it pushing me?' You realize you wouldn't like to be treated that way, so you apologize to your Driver Part, and ask it, 'What are you afraid would happen if you didn't drive me to achieve?' Then you quickly learn that actually your Driver Part is trying to protect you from not achieving and not getting your parents' approval. You know what it feels like to have your parents' disapprove so you thank your Driver Part for wanting to protect you from that discomfort.

You notice how your Driver enjoys hearing your words of thanks, and how you now feel differently towards your Driver Part. In fact, you realize that you feel differently about the rest of your day. Clearer, less stressed, more open to changes and confident that you'll be able to handle whatever happens.

And all of that happened within you, within one minute. Like any person, the more you meet your Parts, the better you get to know them and your Self.

Parts I've Noticed, Promises I've Made

Dreams

I woke from a dream. It was more like a nightmare actually. After images of discomfort, of people and places, some past, some fantasy.

What if my dreams were my Parts breaking through that wall of consciousness I keep so carefully raised through my waking day?

Who were the main characters in my dream? What were their concerns? Their intentions?

How are these key characters similar to Parts of me? Ah, I see their similarities.

Next time I awake from a dream, I'll say 'Hello' to those Parts in my dream.

Be my curious and compassionate Self, and ask them, 'What do you want to tell me?'

That's another way my Self can get to know my Parts.

Example – How do you relate to this?

Have you ever woken up with the remnants of a dream still lingering in your mind? What if you paused for a moment and focused on what you can recall about what happened in your dream?

Perhaps it was a nightmare where you're trying to do a task for some people important to you. And even though you did it, you didn't do it well enough. The people in the dream tell you so. It was so important not to let them down. A wave of embarrassment washes through you, and then helplessness, because you can't change what's happened, and you can't change that you're not smart enough to do the job to the standard that they wanted. That's the moment you woke up feeling like a failure, embarrassed and anxious.

See if you can recall the characters involved and what their concerns and intentions were in relation to you? It's OK if each character isn't that clear. Then ask your Self, 'How are these key characters similar to Parts of me? Perhaps you can see your Fear of Failure Part in your dream making you fearful of failing to do the task perfectly. And then you may recognize the Driver Part that despite how fearful you were, insisted that you go ahead and do the task anyway . But what you may not have been so aware of is how your Pleaser Part also drives you to do things perfectly so that you make people happy, have them like you and get their praise.

By reviewing your dreams, you can discover Parts of you that in your everyday life remain just outside your awareness, but who manifest themselves as characters in the drama of your nighttime dreams.

Self Leadership Road Map

1. Self-Protector Relationship Building

S.I.F.T Parts
Feeling towards Self 😊

8. Thank All Parts

2. Step Aside & Thank

S.I.F.T Parts
Feeling towards Protector?
Appreciate +ve intent

Managers
- Control

Protectors

Fire Fighters
- Out of Control

7. Transform Protectors
What Role do you want to play now Exile healed?

What are you concerned would happen if you didn't do what you do?

3. Self-Exile Relationship Building

S.I.F.T Parts
Feeling towards Exile?
Comfort Exile

Exiles

Earth
Water
Light
Wind
Fire

6. Unburden
Release extreme feelings/beliefs

5. Retrieval
Like to leave past & join me here & now?

4. Witness & Reparent
What would you like to have said / done?

References

Earley, J. (2009). *Self-Therapy: A Step-By-Step Guide to Creating Wholeness and Healing Your Inner Child Using IFS, A New Cutting-Edge Psychotherapy.* Larkspur: Pattern Systems Books.

Earley, J. (2016). *Self-Therapy, Volume 2: A Step-By-Step Guide to Advanced IFS Techniques for Working with Protectors.* Larkspur: Pattern Systems Books.

Earley, J. (2016). *Self-Therapy, Volume 3: A Step-By-Step Guide to Using IFS for Eating Issues, Procrastination, the Inner Critics, Depression, Perfectionism, Anger, Communication, and More.* Larkspur: Pattern Systems Books.

Ecker, B., Ticic, R., & Hulley, L. (2012). *Unlocking the Emotional Brain: Eliminating Symptoms at Their Roots Using Memory Reconsolidation.* New York: Routledge

Goulding, R., & Schwartz, R. (1995). *The Mosaic Mind: Empowering the Tormented Selves of Child Abuse Survivors.* New York: W.W. Norton.

Levine, P.A. (2010). *In an Unspoken Voice: How the Body Releases Trauma and Restores Goodness.* Berkeley: North Atlantic Books.

Rothschild, B. (2003). *The Body Remembers Casebook: Unifying Methods and Models in the Treatment of Trauma and PTSD.* New York: W.W Norton.

Sweezy, M. & Zikind, E., eds. (2013). *Internal Family Systems Therapy: New Dimensions.* New York: Routledge.

Schwartz, R. (1997). *Internal Family Systems.* New York: Guildford Press.

Schwartz, R. (2001). *Introduction to the Internal Family Systems Model.* Oak Park: Trailheads Publications.

Shapiro, F. (2013). *Getting Past your Past: Take Control of Your Life with Self-Help Techniques from EMDR Therapy.* Pennsylvania: Rodale

Shapiro, F. & Forrest. M. F. (1998). *EMDR: The Breakthrough 'Eye Movement' Therapy for Overcoming Anxiety, Stress and Trauma.* New York: Basic Books

Van Der Kolk, B. (2015). The Body Keeps the Score: New York: Penguin Books.

Weiss, B. (2013). *Illustrated Workbook for Freedom from Your Inner Critic: A Self Therapy Approach.* Larkspur: Pattern Systems Books.

Weiss, B. (2013). *Self-Therapy Workbook: An Exercise Book for the IFS Process.* Larkspur: Pattern Systems Books.

www.ingramcontent.com/pod-product-compliance
Lightning Source LLC
Chambersburg PA
CBHW042050290426
44110CB00001B/12